Print information available on the last page

Rev. date: 04/23/2019

To order additional copies of this book, contact:
Xlibris Corporation
1-888-795-4274
www.Xlibris.com
Orders@Xlibris.com

RECIPES
THAT HAVE CREATED
MEMORIES

By
Frances Elwell Ventura

CONTENTS

Introduction

For many years I have been thinking about putting together a cookbook that included some of the Italian cooking recipes of my mother, Ann Giudice. I want to honor her because of all the mouth-watering dishes she made and all the wonderful memories that went with them. The dishes from her kitchen are easy to make, and, even though we did not cook with her, we learned by watching her. Now I would like to share them with you.

Every year, when the family gets together to celebrate the holidays, food is always a delight. There were always special dishes that belonged to each holiday, and our celebrations would not have been the same without them. Even if you haven't ever been to my mother's house for a meal, I hope you can still imagine what it would be like. I will always remember the aroma of meatballs and sauce cooking away first thing on Sunday morning for dinner at noon. On weekdays, my mother always prepared an early dinner as if guests were going to be there, even if there were only two people there.

The recipes in this cookbook are designed to be easy and economical. A few of the methods and ingredients have been adjusted to reduce cooking time. I use only fresh ingredients that can be readily found in a grocery store. For example, I prefer freshly grated cheese to the pre-packaged kind. Even the highest grades of oil can vary in flavor so make sure you choose one that one that suits your palate.

I hope each one of these recipes brings as much pleasure to you as they have to me, whether you are cooking it for the first time or renewing fond memories from your own past.

Buon appetito!

Antipasti

Antipasto, meaning "before the meal," is the traditional first course. Sometimes it can be a full meal in itself, served either hot or cold. It can include anything from Italian cheeses, roasted red peppers, marinated artichokes and fried meatballs to salad dressed with vegetables and oil and vinegar.

Some classic ingredients in an antipasto are artichoke hearts, radishes, pickled beets, tomatoes, fennel, celery, olives, salami, anchovies, prosciutto (sometimes wrapped around melon), salad greens, mushrooms, pepperoni, hard-boiled eggs, boiled potatoes, and green beans.

Leaving the vegetables in large pieces makes it easy to dip them in olive oil. The antipasto can be served at the table instead of a mixed green salad.

Appetizers

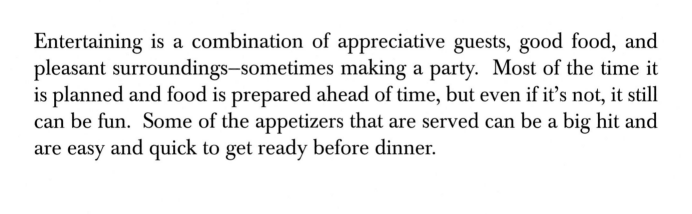

Entertaining is a combination of appreciative guests, good food, and pleasant surroundings—sometimes making a party. Most of the time it is planned and food is prepared ahead of time, but even if it's not, it still can be fun. Some of the appetizers that are served can be a big hit and are easy and quick to get ready before dinner.

ARTICHOKE FRITTERS

Ingredients

    2 cans of artichoke hearts (water packed), drained
    6 large eggs
    1/4 cup olive oil
    1/2 cup Parmesan cheese
    1 cup flour
    1 teaspoon baking powder
    1/4 teaspoon garlic powder
    1 tablespoon dried parsley
    Olive and Crisco vegetable oil, for frying (half olive and half vegetable oil)

Method

1. Cut artichokes into bite-sized pieces.
2. Beat eggs and oil.
3. Add cheese to egg mixture.
4. Mix flour, baking powder, garlic powder, and parsley.
5. Add to egg and cheese mixture. Blend until smooth.
6. Dip artichoke in batter, coating well.
7. Place artichokes into hot oil. If you are using a deep fryer, the basket should be submerged in oil before placing the artichokes. Fry in medium-hot oil until golden brown on both sides. You can fry the fritters in a large, heavy-bottomed frying pan.
8. Drain excess oil from the fritters on paper towels.
9. Serve at room temperature or heat before serving.

No matter how many of these delicious fritters you make, you will never have enough!

CHICKEN STICKS

<u>Ingredients</u>

    3 pounds (about 25 pieces) chicken drumettes or wings
    1 cup (2 sticks) butter or margarine
    1-1/2 cups flour
    1/3 cup of sesame seeds
    1 tablespoon salt
    1/2 tablespoon ground ginger

<u>Method</u>

1.   Wash and drain chicken on a paper towel.
2.   Melt butter or margarine.
3.   Mix flour, sesame seeds, salt, pepper, and ginger in a dish.
4.   Dip chicken pieces one at a time in melted butter. (Let excess butter drip into dish.)
5.   Roll chicken in flour mixture to coat generously; then set aside on sheets of waxed paper until all are coated.
6.   Arrange in pan so that the sticks do not touch.
7.   Bake at 350 degrees for 1 hour or until golden on the bottom.
8.   Slide in heated broiler for 3 to 5 minutes until golden.

PIZZA – BASIC RECIPE

<u>Ingredients</u>

Dough:

1 can evaporated milk
1 can water (use the evaporated milk can)
9 tablespoons sugar
3 tablespoons salt
3 cups cold water (to cool milk mixture)
3 packages of dry yeast (Fleischmann's Active Dry Yeast)
1-1/2 cups warm water (to proof yeast)
1/2 cup vegetable shortening (Crisco) or 1 stick margarine
5 pounds of flour (do not use all 5 pounds at once)

Toppings

Pastene Kitchen Ready or crushed tomatoes or chopped fresh tomatoes
Salt
Pepper
Oregano
Garlic powder
Grated Romano cheese
Shredded mozzarella
Olive oil

<u>Method</u>

1. Heat evaporated milk and 1 can water.
2. Dissolve sugar and salt in milk.
3. Bring to scalding or slow boil; let cool.
4. Add three cups of cold water to cool the milk mixture
5. To proof the yeast, put lukewarm water in a separate bowl; add a pinch of sugar and dry yeast. It is important that the water is not too hot; the water temperature should be 110 degrees. If the water is too hot, the bread will not rise. The yeast should froth.
6. Add yeast mixture to cooled milk. If milk is not cooled, it will kill the yeast.
7. Melt shortening.
8. Place one-third of the flour into a large bowl and stir in all the liquids.
9. Gradually add enough flour until the dough forms a soft ball that no longer clings to the sides of the bowl. Turn it out onto a floured surface.
10. With floured hands, pick up the far edge and fold towards you. Push away from you into the dough with the heel of one hand, and at the same time give the dough a quarter of a turn by pulling it toward you with the other hand. Repeat kneading for 8 to 10 minutes or until dough feels satiny and smooth. Split the dough into two pieces. Place each half of the dough into a large greased bowl, and turn it so the greased side is up. Cover the bowl and set it in a draft free warm place f or 1 to 1-1/2 hours until it doubles in bulk.
11. When it has doubled in bulk, press with two fingers. If indentation stays, the dough is ready.
12. Press dough down and turn onto a floured board.
13. Place a piece of dough onto a greased pizza pan.
14. Spread canned tomatoes or chopped fresh tomatoes on the dough, and sprinkle with salt, pepper, garlic powder, and oregano. Add desired toppings (pepperoni, peppers, onions) and then cheese.
15. Drizzle with olive oil and gently press down so pizza toppings adhere to dough.
16. Bake at 350 degrees for about 15 to 20 minutes. The bottom crust should be golden brown.

It's Saturday night in a hot kitchen and there's a summer breeze. It's pizza night at Grandma Giudice's. There were always at least six pizzas being served, and the leftover dough made yummy fried dough. This is the most flavorful dough recipe.

Makes approximately five to six pizzas.

PIZZA – NEW RECIPE

<u>Ingredients</u>

> 3 cups lukewarm water
> 3 tablespoons sugar
> 3 envelopes yeast
> 1/2 cup olive oil
> 5 teaspoons salt
> 9 cups flour

<u>Method</u>

1. Preheat oven to 350 degrees.
2. Test water on wrist.
3. Combine sugar and water in a large bowl and add yeast.
4. Add 9 cups flour.
5. Follow steps for Pizza – Basic Recipe, starting at step 8.
6. Cook pizza for 15 to 20 minutes.

I can remember my mom kneading dough for pizza and bread. She complained about a sore wrist so she went to the doctor who told her that she had tennis elbow. She was so surprised because she never played tennis, but the doctor said it was just a term they used. We laughed, and years later she still makes pizza dough.

Makes three to four pizzas depending on the thickness of the pizza.

PIZZA PIENA

Ingredients

Dough:

2-1/2 to 3 cups flour
4 heaping teaspoon shortening

3 large eggs
1/2 teaspoon salt
1/2 teaspoon black pepper

Filling:

1 pound ricotta (Dragone or Sorrento)
1 pound fresh, unsalted ricotta cheese
6 large eggs
1 teaspoon salt
1/2 cup grating cheese (Romano)
1/2 pound ham, cubed
1/4 pound salami, cubed
Small pepperoni, skinned/sliced

Method

Dough:

1. Blend flour and shortening, add eggs, salt, and pepper.
2. Mix well. (If too thick, add a few drops of water.)
3. Knead.
4. Cut in half for two crusts.

Filling:

5. Blend both ricotta cheeses, salt, pepper, eggs, and grated cheese.
6. Grease a 9" x 13" pan.
7. Roll out half dough to fit a 9" x 13" pan. Place on bottom and sides.
8. Layer ricotta mixture and meat until you have used all the filling.
9. Top with remaining dough.
10. Cut slits (3 or 4) in top crust.
11. Brush with egg wash (egg and a little water).
12. Bake at 350 degrees for 30 minutes and then at 300 degrees for 40 minutes.

I remember when I was young, I did an errand for the woman upstairs from us, and she rewarded me with a piece of pizza piena. Only special people get this. You don't get a piece unless you really, really like it, says my mom. It is an Easter special.

RICE CROQUETTES

<u>Ingredients</u>

2 tablespoons butter
10 ounces rice (Italian Arborio or regular white), cooked according to directions
1 can chicken broth
2 eggs
6 tablespoons Parmesan cheese
Salt and pepper
Mixture of hamburg (meatball mixture)
1-1/2 cups Italian style breadcrumbs
6 ounces mozzarella cheese, cubed
1-1/2 cups breadcrumbs
Oil for frying

<u>Method</u>

1.   Melt butter in sauce pan.
2.   Add rice and stir for a few minutes.
3.   Add the chicken broth and stir.
4.   Cover and cook until the broth is absorbed.
5.   Set aside and cool.
6.   In a bowl, beat one egg and add the Parmesan cheese, salt, and pepper.
7.   Add this mixture to the cooled rice.
8.   Have meat mixture beside rice, and have the bread crumbs in another plate.
9.   Scoop rice into palm of hand, then a tablespoon of meat, and then a piece
     of mozzarella.
10. Cover that with a spoonful of rice and form into a ball.
11. Roll each ball in beaten egg, and coat with the bread crumbs.
12. Heat the oil, and fry the croquettes until golden brown.
13. Drain well and serve hot, warm or at room temperature.

ROASTED RED PEPPERS

<u>Ingredients</u>

Red peppers
Olive oil
Chopped garlic
Salt and pepper

<u>Method</u>

1.   Place peppers under a broiler until skin is black. (Turn so all sides get black.)
2.   Put in brown paper bag and leave until cool. The paper bag becomes moist, and the skin should come off easily.
3.   Clean (remove core and seeds) and slice red peppers
4.   Place cleaned peppers in a dish. Add olive oil and chopped garlic.
5.   Prepare this ahead of time so that the flavors can mingle.

STUFFED MUSHROOMS

<u>Ingredients</u>

1 pound mushrooms
1/2 cup bread crumbs
1/2 cup grated cheese
2 eggs
1 tablespoon parsley
2 tablespoons olive oil
1/4 teaspoon garlic powder
Salt and pepper
6 tablespoons olive oil

<u>Method</u>

1. Heat oven to 350 degrees.
2. Clean mushrooms, remove stems.
3. Cook stems in a little oil for a few minutes.
4. In a bowl, beat eggs lightly.
5. Add bread crumbs, cheese, parsley, 2 tablespoons of oil, garlic, and salt and pepper to taste.
6. Chop stems finely and add to stuffing mixture. Mix.
7. Fill the mushroom caps. Pour 2 tablespoons of oil in bottom of pan. Place mushrooms in the pan, stuffing side up.
8. Pour the rest of the oil over the top of the mushrooms.
9. Bake at 350 degrees for about 20 minutes. Mushrooms are done when water appears at bottom of the pan.
10. Remove and serve hot.

FRITTATA (OMELATE)

Ingredients

     3 tablespoons olive oil
1/2 cup sliced onions
Salt and pepper to taste
1/3 cup grated cheese (Romano)
1 chopped tomato
5 beaten eggs

Method

1.   Heat oil in a frying pan and sauté onions.
2.   Combine all the rest of ingredients and mix with the eggs.
3.   Turn into the pan and cook over low flame about 10 minutes until the top is set.
4.   When the egg looks cooked enough, place the fry pan under broiler until the top browns a little.

This is a good recipe for a busy day. Add a salad and bread, and then dinner is ready!

Soups

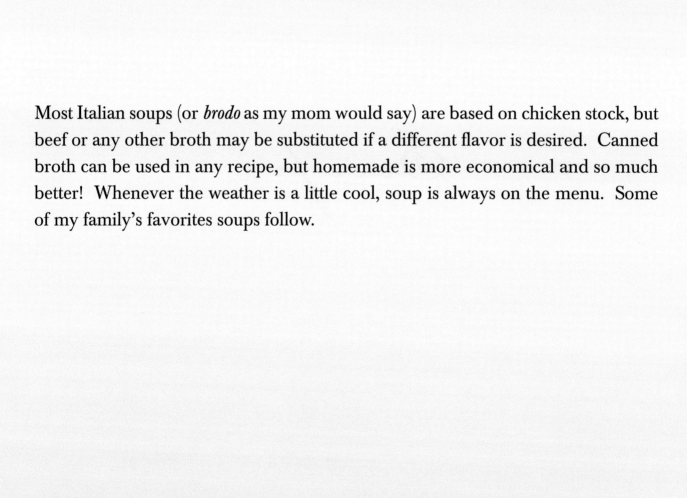

Most Italian soups (or *brodo* as my mom would say) are based on chicken stock, but beef or any other broth may be substituted if a different flavor is desired. Canned broth can be used in any recipe, but homemade is more economical and so much better! Whenever the weather is a little cool, soup is always on the menu. Some of my family's favorites soups follow.

CHICKEN SOUP

<u>Ingredients</u>

One large chicken (remove and wash chicken parts)
4 quarts of water
3 large carrots
1 large onion
3 stalks of celery
1 tomato
Salt
Red pepper flakes (just a few)
Fresh or dried parsley

<u>Method</u>

1. Place the chicken in the water and boil for about an hour or until a little foam surfaces.
2. Scoop off the foam and discard.
3. Add vegetables (whole), salt, pepper, and parsley to the pot.
4. Simmer for another hour or two until the chicken is cooked.
5. Strain the soup and set aside broth.
6. Slice vegetables and add to broth.
7. De-bone chicken and add chicken pieces to broth.
8. If serving the soup with pasta or rice, the pasta and rice should be cooked before adding to soup.

In the old days, my mom would buy a fowl, which is a tough bird, and cook it forever because she said it was the essential ingredient for a good broth. I find cooking a whole chicken or wings and thighs makes a very nice broth as well. Chicken soup is medicine for the soul and a cold. When my mom prepared this soup, it always had great flavor and was wonderfully comforting.

ITALIAN BEAN AND PASTA SOUP (PASTA FAGIOLO)

<u>Ingredients</u>

Olive oil
2 or 3 cloves of garlic, crushed
1 large onion
3 tablespoons of crushed tomatoes or a 14-oz. can of tomatoes
1 teaspoon dried basil
2 cans white cannellini beans (or chickpeas or peas)
Grated Parmesan cheese
1 pound of pasta (ditalini, acini de pepe)

<u>Method</u>

1. Gently fry a large onion and garlic in a little olive oil.
2. Add three tablespoons of crushed tomato and basil.
3. Stir.
4. Simmer sauce before adding beans.
5. Cook pasta in a quart of water.
6. After the pasta is cooked, drain some of the water and add beans and sauce. Simmer.

What a good meal on a cold winter day!

I learned from my husband that in his home town of San Donato, Italy, the entire town celebrates this dish by preparing this dish for the townspeople in the piazza!

LENTIL SOUP (PASTA LENTICCHIE)

<u>Ingredients</u>

    1 package of lentils
    5 carrots
    4 stalks celery
    1 onion
    1 tomato
    1 tablespoon dried parsley
    1 teaspoon salt
    1 teaspoon black pepper
    1/2 cup olive oil
    1/2 pound of small pasta, cooked

<u>Method</u>

Go through lentils; pick out stones or any that are dark.
Put lentils in pot with plenty of cold water, and have a kettle of hot water on the side.
After the first water boils, drain the water and add hot water to the lentils.
Resume the boil.
Add chopped vegetables and cook for about 2 hours.
Add salt and pepper to taste.
Add cooked pasta.

Thick or thin, this soup is a meal in itself.

SMOKED SHOULDER AND MINESTRONE SOUP

Ingredients

    1 smoked shoulder
    Dried minestrone mix (Goodman's or Manichewitz brands)
    Fresh vegetables cut up
    1 can of beans (red kidney or your choice)
    1/4 pound small pasta.

Method

First Meal

1.   Soak shoulder covered with cold water for three days in the refrigerator, changing the water daily.
2.   Place shoulder in a colander over a pot of hot water.
3.   Cook until the bone protrudes, checking the pot and adding hot water as needed. Steaming the shoulder decreases the salt and fat.
4.   When shoulder is cooked, cool and remove outer skin and fat.
5.   Place shoulder in a roasting pan, score it, spread prepared ham glaze, and bake 350 degrees for about an hour.
6.   Cool, slice, and eat.

Second Meal

7.   Leftover ham can be cubed. Break bone so it can fit in stock pot with cold water.
8.   Bring to a boil. Add minestrone mix, cut-up vegetables, beans, and pasta. Uncooked pasta will help thicken the soup.

This vegetable-based soup has a wonderful aroma as it cooks. It is a heartier meal, so no need for a side dish.

Main Dishes

The main dish is generally the only one served unless company is coming. Easy recipes show how some meals are made in minutes. Meat, poultry and fish are some of the choices that can be made with eggs, cheese, and milk. Rice and pasta can also be prepared alone with different sauces at a relatively low cost.

Most of the time, pasta is store-bought, but having it fresh is a treat. Always use plenty of boiling water so that the pasta can move around. One pound will need six quarts, and you should figure on one teaspoon of salt for each quart of water. Always let the water come to a full, rolling boil before adding the pasta. Spaghetti needs to be pushed down in the water as it softens. The length of time needed to cook the pasta will depend on its shape and size. Leftover pasta with sauce can be fried with a little olive oil for a different, tasty meal.

BASIC ITALIAN SAUCE

Ingredients

Olive oil
1 small onion, chopped
2 large cloves garlic, chopped
1 28-ounce can tomatoes (Pastene Kitchen Ready tomatoes)
1 small can tomato paste
Water to fill empty tomato cans
1 tablespoon salt
Pepper
1/4 teaspoon baking soda
1/8 teaspoon crushed red pepper
1 tablespoon dry basil
Fried meatballs or other cooked meat (optional)

Method

1. Pour enough oil to cover the bottom of pan barely.
2. Fry onion until transparent.
3. Add garlic and fry until lightly golden. Do not burn or else spaghetti sauce
    will be bitter.
4. Add tomatoes, paste, and tomato cans of water.
5. Bring to a simmer, and then add baking soda. (Let baking soda foam.)
6. Add salt, pepper, and basil.
7. Add fried meatballs or other cooked meat and simmer over low flame
    for 1-1/2 to 2 hours,
8. Stir occasionally and add hot water if the sauce becomes thick. (Keep a kettle
    of hot water on the stove to use as needed).

You can put this hearty Italian dinner, a Sunday special, on the table without buying a lot of extra ingredients or spending a lot of time. Besides, the lycopene (an antioxidant) battles cancer, heart disease, and high cholesterol.

MARINARA SAUCE

<u>Ingredients</u>

    1/2 cup olive oil
    1 garlic clove (or more), crushed
    1 small onion, sliced
    Salt and pepper
    3 cups crushed tomatoes

<u>Method</u>

1.   Fry the garlic and onion in the olive oil until golden.
2.   Add the tomatoes and cook about 20 minutes.

This sauce is used for pizza and other recipes. It's also delicious with any kind of pasta. It's a base for any number of dishes–parmigiana, fish sauces, and bean dishes. This sauce is mild enough for young children to enjoy.

LASAGNA

Ingredients

Ricotta filling:

2 pounds ricotta
1/2 cup Parmesan grating cheese
1 teaspoon salt
1/8 teaspoon pepper
4 eggs

Other ingredients:

1 pound lasagna noodles
Mozzarella cheese
Marinara sauce (see recipe in this book)
Crushed cooked meatballs (optional) (see recipe in this book)
1 egg, beaten

Method

1. Beat eggs in a bowl, and then add rest of ricotta filling ingredients.
2. Mix until blended.
3. Cook 1 pound of lasagna noodles.
4. Pour sauce into a 9 x 13" or 12 x 15" glass or metal pan with just enough sauce to cover the bottom.
5. Layer lasagna noodles.
6. Place spoonfuls of ricotta filling and crushed meatballs to resemble a checkerboard pattern; place a little extra sauce on top of the crushed meatballs only.
7. Repeat procedure for the second layer except alternate the ricotta filling and crushed meatballs; the second layer of ricotta filling should sit on top of the first layer of crushed meatballs.
8. When finished, top with Parmesan or mozzarella cheese and coat with a beaten egg to seal sauce. Cook at 350 degrees for 25 to 30 minutes.

As a boy, my son Michael used to love to prepare this dish. Even though he could barely reach the counter, he enjoyed doing this. Now that he's a young family man, his choice is to work outside the kitchen.

MANICOTTI SHELLS

Ingredients

Shells:

4 cups flour
4 cups water
4 eggs

Ricotta filling:

2 pounds ricotta cheese
1/2 cup grated Romano cheese

1 teaspoon salt
1/8 teaspoon pepper
1 tablespoon parsley
4 eggs
1-1/2 to 2 pounds spinach
(cooked and drained)

Other:

1 egg, beaten
Marinara sauce (see recipe
in this book)

Method

A paper towel should be soaked in oil and placed in a glass or cup to be used for greasing the skillet when needed.

Shells:

1. Mix all ingredients together with mixer until smooth like pancake batter.
2. Heat a 6-1/2-inch iron skillet until water bounces on it.
3. Grease skillet and then pour a large serving spoon of batter in middle of the skillet. Rotate pan until bottom is covered and batter stops running.
4. Cook over medium heat until sides start to curl and the middle dries to the size of a half-dollar. Then flip over and cook another half minute.
5. Repeat, and pile shells one on top of the other until all the batter is used.

Filling:

1. Mix all ingredients for ricotta filling.
2. Spread a heaping teaspoon of filling in the center of each shell and roll like a jelly roll.
3. Coat a 9 x 13" glass or metal pan with sauce.
4. Lay manicotti in a single layer and pour sauce over them.
5. Place a second layer of manicotti and additional sauce.
6. Lastly, beat an egg and brush it on top to seal in sauce.
7. Bake at 350 degrees for one half hour or until egg is cooked. Remove from oven and allow 15 to 30 minutes before serving.

My son was taught by my mother, and he soon became an expert and now keeps a container of ricotta handy because he never knows when he will be asked to make them. He has patience, but he will work making the shells with two pans and a greased paper towel to get things done more quickly. He'll pile them up 20 at a time!

MEATBALLS

<u>Ingredients</u>

3 pounds ground meat (2 pounds beef, 1/2 pound pork, 1/2 pound veal)
1/2 cup grated Romano cheese
1/2 cup seasoned breadcrumbs
1/2 teaspoon pure garlic powder
1 tablespoon dry parsley
6 eggs
1 teaspoon salt
1/4 teaspoon black pepper
Olive oil

<u>Method</u>

1.   Mix all ingredients together.
2.   Form into balls using ice cream scoop for uniformity.
3.   Heat a very little oil in skillet. Fry meatballs until they are lightly browned
      on both sides and a crust forms.

An alternative to frying: Place meatballs on cookie sheet and bake at 350 degrees (turning to
cook evenly).

BRACCIOLLI

Ingredients

3 slices top round (1/4 thickness)
Olive oil
Marinara sauce (see recipe in
this book)

A. 3 slices salami or chopped
    prosciutto
    2 tablespoons parsley
    2 tablespoons grated cheese
    Salt and pepper to taste

Place a slice of salami on top of
each slice of meat.
Sprinkle parsley, cheese, salt, and
pepper.

B. 3 raw sausages (sliced)
    2 tablespoons parsley
    1 clove garlic or 1/4 tablespoon
    garlic powder
    Salt and pepper to taste

Place 1 portion of sausage meat on
each slice of meat.
Sprinkle parsley, garlic, salt and
pepper.

C. 3 hard boiled eggs (shelled)
    2 tablespoons parsley
    1 tablespoon basil
    1 clove garlic or 1/4 tablespoon
    garlic powder

Place 1 egg on each slice of meat.
Sprinkle with parsley, basil, and garlic.

D. 1/2 pound bacon
    1 tablespoon parsley
    2 cloves garlic or
    1/2 tablespoon garlic powder
    1/2 teaspoon crushed pepper

Blend into paste until smooth using a food processor. Spread some paste on each slice
of meat.

Method

1. Place desired filling as directed above in slice of top round.
2. Roll and secure with round toothpicks (do not use flat toothpicks or string).
3. Fry in oil, browning all sides.
4. Cook in a pot of basic tomato sauce until tender.

Note: Always put the same number of toothpicks in each roll!

GUMBOTTA-ITALIAN STEW

<u>Ingredients</u>

Meat: meatballs, stew meat, or veal cut into small pieces (See recipe in this book)
1 onion
2 cloves garlic
1 small can crushed tomatoes
Four carrots
2 large potatoes
1 cup green peas (or green beans)
1 tablespoon basil

<u>Method</u>

1. Fry meat in a 2 quart sauce pan and put aside.
2. Sauté onion and garlic in the same pan you fried the meat.
3. Add small can of tomatoes and simmer.
4. Cut up carrots, potatoes, and add to mixture.
5. Add meat and peas or beans.
6. Simmer another 30 minutes, and then serve with good crusty Italian bread.

When I was a youngster I never liked this meal and wanted a peanut butter sandwich instead. I would take the vegetables and carefully try to hide them in the napkin. But now I enjoy this meal and look for the vegetables to eat!

CUTLETS PARMIGIANA

Ingredients

    1 pound veal, beef, or chicken cutlets
    2 eggs
    Seasoned breadcrumbs
    Grated cheese
    Mozarella cheese
    Marinara sauce (See the recipe in this book)
    Olive oil

Method

1.   Using a mallet, flatten each cutlet between two sheets of waxed paper.
2.   In a shallow dish, beat the eggs. In another shallow dish, mix the breadcrumbs and grated cheese.
3.   Dip each cutlet in the eggs and then in the breadcrumb mixture.
4.   Fry cutlets in olive oil until lightly brown.
5.   Arrange in a baking dish that has been lightly greased with sauce.
6.   Spoon sauce over each piece and top with slices of mozzarella cheese. Repeat. Bake at 350 degrees until the cheese is melted (about 10 or 15 minutes).

You can prepare the cutlets ahead of time and then reheat before serving, or you can freeze cooked cutlets before making parmigiana.

CHICKEN AMORE

<u>Ingredients</u>

2 pounds boneless chicken (white or dark meat)
1 cup flour
1/4 cup olive oil
4 cloves of garlic
1/4 cup fresh parsley
1/2 teaspoon of poultry seasoning
Salt and pepper
1-1/2 cups of dry white wine
Dash of hot sauce
1 cup of mushrooms (canned or fresh, sliced)
1 7-ounce jar of pimentos or 1 fresh red pepper peeled and sliced
1 can of chicken broth
Egg noodles

<u>Method</u>

1. Season flour with salt, pepper and poultry seasoning.
2. Dredge chicken in flour mixture.
3. Fry chicken in olive oil until golden brown; fry both sides.
4. Remove chicken from pan and drain on paper towels.
5. In the same pan fry garlic then add parsley, hot sauce, and wine.
6. Return chicken to pan and simmer for 35 minutes.
7. Add broth and simmer for 20 more minutes.
8. Serve over buttered noodles.

MEDITERRANEAN CHICKEN

Ingredients

    1 pint grape tomatoes
    16 kalamata olives, pitted and halved
    3 tablespoons drained capers, rinsed
    3 tablespoons olive oil
    4 boneless chicken breast halves
    Salt and pepper

Method

1. Heat oven to 475 degrees.
2. Toss tomatoes, olives, capers, and 2 tablespoons of oil together in a medium bowl, and set aside.
3. Rinse chicken and pat dry.
4. Season both sides with salt and pepper.
5. Heat a large oven-proof skillet over high heat until hot. Add remaining oil and heat until hot but not smoking.
6. Place chicken in skillet and cook until deep golden brown, about four minutes.
7. Turn chicken over, and add tomato mixture.
8. Transfer skillet to oven and cook until chicken is cooked through and tomatoes have softened (about 18 minutes).

CHICKEN MARSALA

Ingredients

       3 pounds boneless chicken, cut up into bite-sized pieces
       1 pound fresh mushrooms, sliced
       2 tablespoons olive oil
       2 tablespoons butter
       1/2 teaspoon crushed rosemary
       2 onions, chopped
       1/2 cup Marsala wine
       1/2 teaspoon thyme
       Salt and pepper to taste

Method

1. Preheat the oven to 350 degrees.
2. Sauté the chicken in olive oil and butter in an uncovered skillet, turning once until light brown on both sides.
3. Add the rosemary, onions, mushrooms and salt and pepper.
4. Drain excess fat.
5. Add the wine and thyme.
6. Cook for 45 minutes.

If you prefer, add your choice of fresh vegetables (I like peas) after adding wine and thyme.

CHICKEN CACCIATORE (HUNTER'S STYLE)

<u>Ingredients</u>

4 pounds cut-up fryer or 2 pounds chicken breast or thighs
1 pound fresh mushrooms, coarsely sliced
1 large green pepper, chopped
1 28-ounce can crushed tomatoes
1 clove garlic
1/2 teaspoon oregano
1/4 cup chopped onion
1/2 cup flour
1 teaspoon salt
1/2 cup olive oil
Dash of crushed red pepper
1/2 cup sweet Marsala wine

<u>Method</u>

1. Put the flour and salt in a resealable plastic bag.
2. Place a few pieces of the chicken in the bag at a time and shake to coat.
3. Heat oil in a heavy-bottomed Dutch oven, put chicken in, and brown it on all sides. You may have to do this in several batches. Remove chicken and set aside.
4. Brown the mushrooms and peppers in the same pan that the chicken was browned in. Set peppers and mushrooms aside.
5. In the same drippings, brown the onion and garlic.
6. Add tomatoes, salt, and red pepper, and simmer for 10 minutes.
7. Add the chicken and the wine.
8. Simmer for 30 minutes or until the chicken is tender.
9. Add the mushrooms, green pepper, peas, and oregano.
10. Simmer for another 5 minutes.

Serve over pasta.

POTATO GNOCCHI

Ingredients

    Flour (see method, varies by size of potato)
    1 potato per person
    2 eggs for about every five potatoes
    Grated Parmesan cheese
    1 teaspoon salt
    Marinara sauce (See recipe in this book)

Method

1. Bake potato then set aside to cool off.
2. On board, place flour and make indent in center and place potato.
3. Beat eggs.
4. Sprinkle a little cheese on the potato and place eggs in the indent, too.
5. Bring enough flour into center to create dough.
6. Knead until all dough is worked together.
7. Roll pieces into one-inch-wide ropes and cut one-inch pieces.
8. Press lightly with a fork to form gnocchi.
9. Drop gnocchi into salted water to which oil has been added.
10. When they float to the top, drain transfer to baking dish.
11. Toss with sauce.
12. Put grated cheese on top, cover with foil, and bake for 20 minutes in a 375-degree oven.

This was a favorite meal made by my sister-in-law Carolina. She would make this meal anytime you were visiting–even if you just went to have coffee.

LINGUINI WITH CLAMS

<u>Ingredients</u>

    4 tablespoons olive oil
    2 cloves garlic (chopped fine)
    2 cans Snow's minced clams with liquid (chopped finely)
    1 pound linguini
    1-1/2 tablespoons minced parsley
    1/2 teaspoon crushed red pepper
    Romano cheese
    1 teaspoon salt
    Pepper

<u>Method</u>

1. In a large skillet, sauté garlic in oil.
2. Add clams and liquid, and continue to cook for 5 to 8 minutes.
3. Add minced parsley, salt, pepper, and red pepper.
4. In the meantime, cook linguini in boiling salted water for about 6 minutes.
    Drain thoroughly.
5. Add linguini to sauce and toss.
6. Sprinkle with grated Romano cheese.

QUICK EASY CRAB CAKES

<u>Ingredients</u>

    1 cup boiling water
    1 box (6 ounces) of corn bread stuffing (Stove Top)
    3 eggs, slightly beaten
    2 16 ounce packages of crabmeat (imitation crabmeat can be used,
    just be sure to squeeze out the water)
    1 stick unsalted butter
    Unflavored bread crumbs (for coating crab cakes)

<u>Method</u>

1. In a bowl, mix together everything except for the butter.
2. Form patties and coat with crumbs.
3. In a heavy skillet, melt 3 tablespoons butter, frying patties until golden brown on both sides.
4. Repeat as needed, adding fresh butter to each batch.

SEAFOOD AGLIO E OLIO

Ingredients

    Olive oil
    1 8 ounce can chopped black olives (pitted)
    1 can clams (fresh is better)
    1 small can anchovies
    1 pound cleaned large shrimp, raw
    1 pound spaghetti or linguine
    Crushed red pepper to taste

Method

1. Sauté garlic in olive oil.
2. Add olives, anchovies, clams, shrimp, and cook for few minutes.
3. Boil pasta, drain, and reserve a little of the water.
4. Add pasta to sauce in pan with shrimp and clams with red pepper.
5. The water that is reserved can be used to add to the mixture if it becomes too dry.

SQUID SAUCE (CALAMARI)

Ingredients

One and a half pounds of fresh squid (cleaned)
1 28-ounce can of crushed tomatoes
1 tablespoon fresh or dried basil
One small onion, finely chopped
Four or five cloves of garlic, minced
Olive oil
Red pepper flakes
Spaghetti, fettuccini, or other similar pasta

Method

1.   Gently fry onion and garlic.
2.   Add tomatoes, basil, and red pepper flakes, and simmer for 30 minutes.
3.   Add squid to sauce, and simmer an additional 30 minutes.
4.   Cook spaghetti according to directions.
5.   Mix sauce and spaghetti and serve.

Grated cheese is not typically served with seafood pasta dishes like this one.

Christmas Eve would not be complete without this traditional dish. It is typically served as part of the evening's menu of seven fishes or seafood dishes.

STUFFED FLOUNDER (FARCITO PESCE)

Ingredients

2 pounds of flounder (or sole)
12 ounces of fresh clams, chopped (can use canned clams)
3/4 cup Italian-flavored breadcrumbs
Juice of one lemon
1/2 cup (one stick) unsalted butter, melted
1/2 cup of grated Romano cheese
Paprika

Method

1.   Pre-heat oven to 350 degrees.
2.   Butter pan.
3.   Wash fish under cold water and pat dry.
4.   Mix clams, breadcrumbs, lemon juice, melted butter, and grated Romano cheese.
5.   Place a spoon full of stuffing on a piece of fish and roll up.
6.   Place fish seam down on buttered pan.
7.   Sprinkle paprika on top of fish.
8.   Bake for 25 minutes.

You can also use haddock, but instead of rolling the filling in the fish, sandwich the stuffing between two pieces of haddock.

TUNA CASSEROLE

<u>Ingredients</u>

    1/2 cup chopped onion
    1 can condensed cream of mushroom soup
    2/3 cup evaporated milk
    1/3 cup grated Parmesan cheese
    1 large can tuna fish
    3 ounces broiled mushrooms, sliced
    1/2 cup chopped black olives
    2 tablespoons minced parsley
    2 teaspoons fresh lemon juice
    Paprika
    6 ounces noodles

<u>Method</u>

1. Cook onion in small amount of hot oil until tender; do not let the onion get brown.
2. Add soup, milk, and cheese; heat and stir.
3. Break tuna in chunks; add it and the remaining ingredients to the pan.
4. Pour into greased 2-quart casserole dish.
5. Sprinkle with additional Parmesan cheese and paprika.
6. Top with minced parsley and olives if desired.
7. Bake in moderate oven at 375 degrees 20 to 25 minutes.
8. Serve with lemon wedges.

BACON AND BAKED BEANS

<u>Ingredients</u>

     2 28-ounce cans of baked beans
     1/2 cup brown sugar
     1/2 cup ketchup
     1/2 package bacon, cooked and crumbled

<u>Method</u>

1.   Heat oven to 350 degrees.
2.   Mix all ingredients in a pot and bake for an hour.

These taste homemade but have to be much faster because nowadays we don't have the time that we did back in the days when we were home all day Saturday. A Saturday night special was baked beans, hot dogs, and fried brown bread.

EGGPLANT PARMIGIANA

Ingredients

    1 smooth large eggplant
    Salt
    2 large eggs
    Seasoned breadcrumbs
    Olive oil
    1/2 recipe marinara sauce (See recipe in this book)
    Mozzarella cheese, sliced

Method

1. Peel and slice eggplant into 1/2-inch thick slices; salt lightly.
2. Place between paper towels for half of an hour or more; place weights (e.g., cans) on top of the slices.
3. In a shallow bowl, beat the eggs. Put the breadcrumbs in another bowl.
4. Dip each slice of eggplant in the egg and then coat both sides with breadcrumbs.
5. Fry in olive oil until both sides are golden brown.
6. Arrange in a baking dish which has been lightly greased with sauce.
7. Spoon sauce over each piece, and top with slices of mozzarella cheese.
8. Bake at 350 degrees until the cheese is melted (about 10 or 15 minutes).

Mozzarella cheese is rich in phosphorus, calcium, and other nutrients. It also replenishes cavity-fighting enamel.

FETTUCINI ALFREDO

Ingredients

    2 cups (1 pound) ricotta cheese
    1/2 cup grated Parmesan cheese
    1-1/2 cups of butter (use less if desired)
    2/3 cup of all-purpose cream or heavy cream
    1 box fettuccini (1/2-inch wide), cooked (12 ounces)
    Salt and pepper to taste

Method

1.   Melt ricotta, grated cheese, butter, and cream over low flame, stirring constantly (do not brown).
2.   Add salt and pepper to taste.
3.   After blended and gently bubbling, pour mixture over cooked fettuccini noodles and toss.

My mother read an article in the Boston Globe about Jackie Kennedy's visit to an Italian restaurant in the North End. She commented that the restaurant made the best Fettuccini Alfredo she had ever tasted. Our mother called the restaurant for the recipe, but they refused to give it to her. Through trial and error, my mother developed this recipe that we are sure is every bit as delicious as the dish eaten by the First Lady!

LINGUINI WTH BROCCOLI

<u>Ingredients</u>

> 2 cloves of garlic
> Olive oil
> 1 tablespoons parsley
> Crushed red pepper to taste
> 2 packages frozen broccoli
> 1 pound linguini
> Grated Romano cheese

<u>Method</u>

1. Sauté garlic in skillet with oil, adding parsley, salt, and red pepper.
2. After simmering, add frozen broccoli. Let cook until light in color.
3. Let sit while cooking the linguini.
4. Cook linguini according to directions, reserving a little of the cooking water.
5. Add pasta and reserved water (as needed) to the skillet.
6. Serve with Romano cheese.

This dish was always a last-minute meal and was one that the whole family liked.

PUMPKIN BREAD

<u>Ingredients</u>

       2/3 cup vegetable shortening (Crisco)
       2-3/4 cups sugar
       4 eggs
       1 can pumpkin filling
       2/3 cup water
       3 1/3 cups flour
       1 1/2 tsp salt
       2 teaspoons baking soda
       1/2 teaspoon baking powder
       1 teaspoon cinnamon
       1 teaspoon cloves
       2/3 cup walnuts nuts (optional)
       2/3 cup raisins

<u>Method</u>

1. Heat oven to 350 degrees.
2. Grease and flour two loaf pans.
3. Cream shortening and sugar.
4. Add eggs, pumpkin, and water.
5. Blend in dry ingredients except nuts and raisins.
6. Add nuts and raisins.
7. Bake in prepared pans until inserted toothpick comes out clean, approximately 30 minutes.

WHOLE WHEAT BREAD

<u>Ingredients</u>

8 to 8-1/2 cups whole wheat flour
2 envelopes Fleischmann's rapid rise yeast
2-1/2 teaspoons salt
1-1/2 cups water
1-1/2 cups milk
1/4 cup vegetable oil
1/4 cup honey

<u>Method</u>

1.	In a large bowl, combine 3-1/2 cups flour, undissolved yeast, and salt.
2.	Heat water, milk, honey, and oil until very warm (120 to 130 degrees).
3.	Gradually add to flour mixture.
4.	Beat for two minutes at medium speed, scraping bowl occasionally.
5.	Add 1 cup of flour, and beat for two minutes at high speed, scraping bowl occasionally.
6.	With spoon, stir in enough of the remaining flour to make a soft dough.
7.	Knead on lightly floured surface until smooth and elastic (about 8 minutes).
8.	Place in greased bowl, turning to grease top.
9.	Cover and let rise in warm place until doubled in size (about 1 hour).
10.	Punch dough down. Let rise again until doubled in size.
11.	Remove dough to lightly floured surface and divide in half.
12.	Shape dough into loaves and put into greased loaf pans.
13.	Let rise again in loaf pans.
14.	Bake at 375 degrees for about 45 minutes.

ZEPPELLAS

Ingredients

    2-1/2 cups flour
    1 package of dry yeast (Fleischmann's rapid rise yeast)
    Vegetable oil for frying
    1/2 tsp salt
    1 cup lukewarm water (about 110 degrees)
    Raisins (Sun Maid) (as much as you like)

Method

1. Place yeast, salt, and water in a mixing bowl. Yeast mixture should froth. See description in pizza dough recipe.
2. Gradually mix in flour.
3. Add raisins, if desired.
4. Knead it, using mixer's dough hook, or for about 10 minutes. The dough should be soft and sticky.
5. Cover dough and let stand for 30 minutes.
6. Set an electric frying pan at 375 degrees with 3 inches of oil.
7. Wet your fingertips with a little oil, which makes handling the sticky dough a little easier.
8. Take a small amount of dough (tablespoon) at a time and drop it in the hot oil. You can use one tablespoon to scoop up the dough and a second to push the dough into the oil. (The dough will be very sticky).
9. Fry until brown on all sides.

This makes a special treat for Christmas Eve.

Desserts

(Dolci)

The end of the meal is the best part for me because I am a person who craves sweets, and desserts–or *dolci*–are pure gratification. Traditional homemade sweets and cakes continue to be favorites after any meal or on any special occasion even without a meal. Any kind of baking requires a certain amount of care and precision in quantities and cooking times that must be followed strictly. Keep in mind that when you serve a hearty meal, you serve a light dessert. A hearty dessert, such as pudding and rich cake, is a perfect ending for a light meal.

ALMOND BISCOTTI

Ingredients

    1 cup sugar
    1/2 teaspoon cloves
    1 cup brown sugar
    1 teaspoon baking powder
    2 large eggs
    1/3 cup vegetable oil (Crisco)
    2 teaspoons cinnamon
    2 tablespoons water
    2-1/2 cups flour
    3 cups almonds, chopped
    1 egg yolk
    1 teaspoon water

Method

1. Preheat oven to 375 degrees.
2. Grease a large cookie sheet.
3. In a blender or food processor, mix all ingredients except the flour and almonds. The mixture should be very creamy.
4. Transfer creamy mixture into a large mixing bowl.
5. Mix in flour and almonds. It's easiest to use your hands because the batter is stiff. If the batter is too stiff, add a few drops of cold water.
6. Let mixture rest for about 5 minutes.
7. Divide dough into six equal portions. Shape the dough into logs on the cookie sheet.
8. Mix egg yolk with 1 teaspoon of water. Brush the yolk mixture on the logs of dough.
9. Bake for 20 minutes. The tops of the cookie should look cracked and dry.
10. Let cookies cool on the cookie sheet until completely cooled.
11. Cut logs diagonally with a serrated knife.

Our mother always hid these cookies in a tin in the dining room in hopes that we would forget about them since these cookies would taste better as they aged. They're quite hard and are ideal for dunking in coffee or wine!

ANISETTE BISCOTTI

Ingredients

    3 eggs
    1 cup sugar
    3 teaspoons baking powder
    2-1/2 cups flour
    1/4 cup milk
    1/2 teaspoon anise oil (not extract) (found at most Italian markets)
    1/2 cup oil

Method

1.   Pre-heat oven to 350 degrees.
2.   Beat eggs.
3.   Add sugar, milk, anise oil, and oil.
4.   Mix baking powder and flour together, add to egg mixture, and blend until mixed.
5.   Form three loaves and place on greased cookie sheet.
6.   Bake in oven for 10 minutes. When golden brown, remove them from oven and cool slightly. Then cut them into slices diagonally.
7.   Place back on cookie sheet and toast for a few minutes until light brown.
8.   If you wish, you may use frosting and not toast cookies after cutting them diagonally.

When these cookies were being cut before they were toasted, my mom would pile the ends in a dish. Anybody who was there would always move close to her to get them while they were still hot.

ANISETTE EASTER COOKIES

Ingredients

    3/4 cups shortening
    2-1/2 cups sugar
    4 eggs
    6-1/2 cups flour
    7 teaspoons baking powder
    1 cup milk
    1 teaspoon anise oil
    Colored candy sprinkles

Method

1. Heat oven to 375 degrees.
2. Cream shortening and sugar until creamy.
3. Stir in eggs one at a time.
4. Sift together flour and baking powder.
5. Add anise oil to milk.
6. Alternately add flour and milk to egg mixture and mix well.
7. Batter will be stiff.
8. Form balls the size of walnuts and place on a greased cookie sheet
9. Bake in 375-degree oven until light brown.
10. Frost (when cool) with white icing, and sprinkle with colored candies.
    (See Recipe for decorating icing in this book)

Easter joy! We all love these cookies and they taste as good as they look. A small ice cream scoop will make the cookies come out uniform.

EASTER COOKIE BASKETS

Ingredients

    6 cups flour
    6 large eggs
    2 tablespoons baking powder
    1 cup Crisco
    1-3/4 cups sugar
    1 teaspoon pure vanilla
    8 hard-boiled eggs
    Frosting
    Marshmallow peeps
    Jellybeans

Method

1.   Pre-heat oven to 350 degrees.
2.   Mix all ingredients except for the hard-boiled eggs.
3.   Divide dough into eight balls.
4.   Flatten each ball of dough and cut out a semi-circle to create the handle of the basket. Save this extra dough. You use it to secure the egg to the basket.
5.   Place hard-boiled egg (with shell on) on the raw dough below the handle of the basket.
6.   Using the dough that was cut out to create the handle, cut in half and roll two rope-like pieces. Secure the egg to the basket with the two pieces of dough (make a cross over the hard-boiled egg).
7.   Bake in oven until light brown.
8.   Frost when cool, and place jellybeans and marshmallow peep on frosting. (See decorating icing recipe in this book).

The grandchildren always love to help decorate, but my Mom has a certain way to place everything on the cookies just right--and those are the ones that she gives away. She would make about 50 or so.

Makes 8 baskets of 8 ounces each.

SESAME SEED COOKIES (BISCOTTI DI REGINA)

<u>Ingredients</u>

    2 sticks of butter
    4 eggs, beaten
    1/4 cup milk
    5 teaspoons baking powder
    2 cups sugar
    2 teaspoons vanilla
    5 cups of sifted flour
    Sesame seeds

<u>Method</u>

1. Cream butter and sugar.
2. Add beaten eggs, vanilla, flour, and baking powder.
3. Slowly add milk to the mixture and mix well.
4. Place sesame seeds on waxed paper.
5. Make little balls of the dough and roll in the sesame seeds.
6. Place on a greased cookie sheet.
7. Bake in a 400-degree oven for 15 minutes.

These were a family favorite!

CHOCOLATE SPICE BALLS

Ingredients

      6 tablespoons baking powder
      2 teaspoons cinnamon
      3 teaspoons allspice
      1 teaspoon black pepper
      5 pounds flour
      2 pounds sugar
      1 pound margarine or shortening
      1 pound whole walnuts
      1 box dark raisins
      12 ounces chocolate pieces
      1 quart milk
      8 large eggs
      14 tablespoons cocoa

Method

1.   Pre-heat oven to 350 degrees.
2.   Mix shortening and flour.
3.   Add remaining ingredients and mix.
4.   Form balls of dough using a small ice cream scoop.
5.   Place balls of dough on greased cookie sheets.
6.   Cook until golden brown.
7.   Frost with chocolate frosting. (See recipe for decorating icing in this book)

FIG-FILLED COOKIES (CUCCIDATI)

<u>Ingredients</u>

Dough:

6 cups sifted all-purpose flour
2 teaspoons baking powder
1 teaspoon baking soda
1/2 teaspoon salt
1 cup shortening
2 cups sugar
2 eggs
1 teaspoon vanilla
1 cup sour cream

Filling:

2 pounds figs, chopped
1 pound raisins
1/2 pound shelled walnuts
Small container orange peel
Small container lemon peel
2 cups orange juice

<u>Method</u>

Dough:

1. Sift together flour, baking powder, baking soda, and salt.
2. Work shortening in a bowl until creamy.
3. Add sugar; blend well.
4. Add eggs and vanilla; blend well.
5. Stir in sour cream.
6. Add dry ingredients a little at a time, mixing after each addition.
7. Cover mixture and chill one hour.

Filling:

8. Combine all ingredients with a meat grinder, using orange juice to prevent sticking.

Preparation:

9. Heat oven to 425 degrees.
10. Roll out dough in small portions to 1/8-inch thick on lightly floured board; cut with a 3-inch scalloped cookie cutter.
11. Place the circles one inch apart on ungreased cookie sheet.
12. Spoon 1 teaspoon of filling in the center of each circle, moisten edges with water, and place a top circle of dough over the filling. Use a fork to seal edges.
13. Bake 8 to 10 minutes; cool on wire racks.

A Christmas special! These cookies are good. Not only can you figure out that this fruit is loaded with nutrients that are good for you, but it's very tasty, too!

HALF-MOON COOKIES

<u>Ingredients</u>

    3 cups sifted flour
    1 teaspoon baking powder
    1 teaspoon baking soda
    1/2 teaspoon salt
    3/4 cup shortening
    1-1/2 cups sugar
    2 eggs
    1 teaspoon vanilla
    1 cup sour cream

<u>Method</u>

1.   Sift the first four ingredients together.
2.   Cream shortening and sugar.
3.   Beat eggs and vanilla.
4.   Add to creamed mixture.
5.   Add dry ingredients alternating with sour cream.
6.   Drop by tablespoon (or small ice cream scoop) onto greased cookie sheet.
7.   Bake 12 to 15 minutes in a 350-degree oven. Cool.
8.   Frost one half (of the flat side) with chocolate and the other with white/vanilla frosting. (See recipe for decorating icing in this book).

HOLIDAY OATMEAL COOKIES

<u>Ingredients</u>

1 cup butter
1 cup sugar
1 cup brown sugar
2 eggs
1 teaspoon vanilla
2 cups sifted flour
1 teaspoon baking soda
3/4 teaspoon salt
3 cups uncooked quick oats
1/2 cup nuts
1 cup chocolate pieces or colored candies.

<u>Method</u>

1. Cream butter and sugar until fluffy.
2. Blend in eggs and vanilla.
3. Sift flour, soda and salt.
4. Add to creamed mixture.
5. Stir in nuts, oats, and chips.
6. Drop onto greased cookie sheets by ice cream scoop.
7. Bake at 350 degrees for 10 to 12 minutes.
8. Cool on wire racks.

PIZZELLE

Ingredients

  6 eggs
  3-1/2 cups flour
  1-1/2 cups sugar
  1 cup margarine, melted and cooled but still liquid
  4 teaspoons baking powder
  2 tablespoons vanilla or anise
  Confectioner's sugar

You will need a pizzelle (waffle) iron for this recipe. Many Italian food stores sell this appliance.

Method

1.   Beat eggs, adding sugar gradually, and beat until smooth.
2.   Add margarine and vanilla or anise.
3.   Sift flour and baking powder
4.   Add to egg mixture.
5.   Dough will be sticky enough to be dropped by tablespoon onto a pizzelle machine.
6.   Sprinkle cooked pizzelle with confectioner's sugar if desired.

Thin, crispy, and delicious!

LADY FINGERS (GEMELLI)

<u>Ingredients</u>

1.   8 eggs
   1 cup milk
   1 pound Crisco
   3 cups sugar

2.   8 cups flour
   8 teaspoons baking powder
   2 teaspoons lemon juice

Powdered sugar in a small bowl or dish

<u>Method</u>

1. Mix ingredients under (1) together very well, for about 10 minutes.
2. Then add to the mixture the ingredients under (2).
3. Grease cookie sheets with Crisco or Pam spray.
4. Take one tablespoon of dough, and roll it in the powdered sugar.
5. Place on sheet.
6. Bake at 400 degrees for 8 to 10 minutes.

This recipe is from my cousin Connie, who always baked them for her parties. Instead of waiting for her to make them, we just had to have the recipe!

NEW ENGLAND HERMITS

Ingredients

6 eggs
1/2 cup butter
1/2 cup sugar
2 eggs
1/2 cup molasses
2 cups sifted flour
1/2 teaspoon salt
3/4 teaspoon baking soda
3/4 teaspoon cream of tartar
1 teaspoon ground cinnamon
1/2 teaspoon ground cloves
1/4 teaspoon nutmeg
1/8 teaspoon ground allspice
3 tablespoons chopped citron
1/2 cup chopped raisins
1/2 cup currants
1/4 cup chopped walnuts

Method

1.   Cream butter with sugar until light and fluffy.
2.   Beat in eggs and molasses.
3.   Sift together flour, salt, baking soda, cream of tartar, and spices.
4.   Stir dry mixture into creamed mixture.
5.   Stir in citron, raisins, currants, and nuts.
6.   Spread batter evenly into greased 13" by 9" by 2" pan.
7.   Bake at 350 degrees for about 20 minutes.
8.   Set pan on rack to cool, cutting 3" by 1" bars while slightly warm.
9.   Cool completely before removing from pan.

SNICKERDOODLES

Ingredients

    1/2 cup butter
    1/2 cup shortening
    1-1/2 cups sugar
    2 eggs
    1 teaspoon vanilla
    2-2/3 cups sifted flour
    2 teaspoons cream of tartar
    1 teaspoon baking soda
    1/4 teaspoon salt
    2 tablespoons sugar
    1 teaspoon ground cinnamon

Method

1. Beat butter and shortening until light.
2. Add sugar and beat until fluffy.
3. Beat in eggs and vanilla.
4. Sift together flour, cream of tartar, baking soda, and salt.
5. Add to beaten mixture.
6. Combine 2 tablespoons sugar and cinnamon in a small dish.
7. Shape dough into small balls, about 1" round, and roll in sugar and cinnamon mixture.
8. Place about 2" apart on ungreased cookie sheets.
9. Bake at 400 degrees for 8 to 10 minutes.

My children always enjoyed these cookies as an after school snack. Cinnamon is an old spice with a new twist. It battles food poisoning, heart disease, and ulcers. It also encourages healthy eating!

STAINED GLASS COOKIES

Ingredients

> 12 ounces chocolate pieces
> 1/2 cup butter
> 1 package tiny marshmallows
> 1/2 cup chopped nuts
> Bag of coconut

Method

1. Melt chocolate and butter on low heat; let stand until cool.
2. In a bowl, mix marshmallows and nuts.
3. Cut 2 pieces of wax paper 14" long; sprinkle with additional nuts or coconut.
4. Mix marshmallows and nuts with mixture.
5. Place on waxed paper and shape into logs, then wrap in foil. Place in freezer.
6. Unwrap and slice (frozen) when ready to serve.

The children would always have a hand in making this special Christmas treat.

DECORATING ICING

<u>Ingredients</u>

    2 pounds confectionery sugar
    1 cup shortening
    3/4 cup milk
    Pinch of salt
    1 teaspoon of vanilla
    1 tablespoon of cocoa for chocolate

<u>Method</u>

Mix all ingredients together at high speed in mixer until creamy.

My sister Anita is the cake decorator in the family. She has decorated many cakes for important people, including a President of the United States! As hard as the rest of us try, we can't come close to match her talent. When the children were little, she would always give them some frosting by placing a drop on their nose to lick off.

CARROT CAKE

Ingredients

Cake:

2 cups flour
1-1/2 teaspoons baking powder
2 teaspoons baking soda
1 teaspoon salt
1 teaspoon vanilla
2 teaspoons cinnamon
Dash lemon juice
4 eggs
2 cups sugar

1-1/4 cup oil
2 cups grated carrots
8 ounces crushed drained pineapple
3 to 4 ounces chopped walnuts
3 to 4 ounces shredded coconut
3 to 4 ounces raisins

Frosting:

8 ounces cream cheese
1 stick margarine
1 cup confectionery sugar

Method

1.   Measure all dry ingredients. Set aside.
2.   Beat eggs.
3.   Add sugar and oil and mix.
4.   Add carrots, pineapple, walnuts, coconut, and raisins to egg mixture.
5.   Mix well.
6.   Add dry ingredients.
7.   Bake for one hour at 350 degrees.
8.   Prepare frosting by beating all ingredients together until smooth.
9.   Once the cake is completely cool, frost with cream cheese frosting and garnish with shredded carrots.

My sister Lucia had to wait four years before a college friend would give her this recipe!

CHEESECAKE

<u>Ingredients</u>

Graham cracker crust (prepare according to package directions)
5 eggs, separated
1 cup sugar
1 tablespoon sugar
1 pound (16 ounces) cream cheese at room temperature
1 cup sour cream
2 tablespoons flour
1 teaspoon vanilla extract
Berries (any kind works)

<u>Method</u>

1. Heat oven to 275 degrees.
2. Butter a 9-inch spring-form pan.
3. Prepare graham cracker crust according to package directions and press into the bottom and sides of the spring-form pan.
4. Prepare filling by beating yolks until thick and lemon-colored.
5. Gradually beat in sugar.
6. Break up cream cheese; add to egg mixture, beating until smooth.
7. Add sour cream, flour, and vanilla.
8. Beat egg whites until stiff (that is, until it holds a peak) but not dry.
9. Gently fold into cream cheese mixture.
10. Pour filling into prepared pan.
11. Bake 70 minutes.
12. Turn off oven and leave in one hour without opening oven door.
13. Remove from oven and cool.
14. Remove cheesecake from pan just before serving and top with fruit.

It is best to make this cake one full day prior to serving and allow it to refrigerate overnight.

CHOCOLATE WONDER CAKE

Ingredients

    1-1/2 cups flour
    1 cup sugar
    1/2 teaspoon salt
    1/2 teaspoon baking soda
    1/2 teaspoon baking powder
    3 tablespoons unsweetened cocoa
    1 teaspoon vanilla
    1 tablespoon white vinegar
    6 tablespoons oil
    1 cup water
    Decorating icing (See recipe in this book)

Method

1.   Pre-heat oven to 350 degrees.
2.   Mix dry ingredients in cake pan.
3.   Make three holes in this mixture.
4.   Pour vanilla in the first hole, vinegar in the second, and oil in the third.
5.   Pour the water over the mixture and mix well with a fork.
6.   Bake for 20 minutes or until inserted toothpick comes out clean.
7.   Frost the cake when it is still warm and in the plan. Serve directly from the pan.

When we were growing up, this was a dessert my mom would make for us. We were always surprised at how good this cake would look and taste after it was baked. She would always frost it right in the pan with vanilla frosting and serve it warm.

CHOCOLATE CAKE MADE IN A HEARTBEAT

<u>Ingredients</u>

      1 box chocolate cake mix
      4 large eggs
      1-1/2 cups water
      1/2 cup vegetable oil
      1 teaspoon vanilla
      1 can chocolate frosting

<u>Method</u>

1.   Mix all ingredients and bake at 350 degrees for 50 minutes.
2.   Cool the cake completely before the glaze is drizzled over the cake.

This recipe is fast and delicious! The secret to chocolate glaze is to melt one can of chocolate frosting in the microwave until it's pourable. It looks good and covers any cracks or smudges, no matter what kind of dessert it is.

COFFEE CAKE

Ingredients

  2 cups sifted all-purpose flour
  1-1/2 teaspoons baking powder
  1/2 teaspoon baking soda
  1 teaspoon salt
  1 cup butter
  1-1/4 cups sugar
  1 teaspoon vanilla extract
  2 eggs
  1 cup sour cream
  1 cup chopped walnuts
  1 teaspoon ground cinnamon
  2 tablespoons sugar
  1/3 cup orange juice
  2 tablespoons dark brown sugar

Method

1.   Heat oven to 350 degrees.
2.   Grease a 10-inch tube pan.
3.   Sift flour, baking powder, baking soda, and salt together.
4.   Blend butter and 1-1/4 cups sugar in a large bowl; beat until mixture is light and fluffy.
5.   Add vanilla and eggs one at a time, beating well after each addition.
6.   Blend in sour cream.
7.   Gradually add sifted dry ingredients to creamed mixture and beat until well blended.
8.   Spoon half of the batter into prepared pan.
9.   Mix nuts, cinnamon, and the remaining 2 tablespoons of sugar; sprinkle half of the mixture over batter in pan.
10.   Top with remaining batter and sprinkle with remaining mixture.
11.   With a knife, cut through batter several times to marble slightly.
12.   Bake 45 to 50 minutes, and cool on wire rack 10 minutes.
13.   Remove from pan and place on serving plate.
14.   Combine orange juice and the 2 tablespoons brown sugar in a saucepan; cook over low heat until sugar is dissolved. Brush over top and sides of warm cake. Serve warm.

RUM CAKE

Ingredients

1 box yellow/gold cake mix, made
according to box directions
and cooled
1 can evaporated milk, with
water added to equal one quart
of liquid
1-1/2 cups sugar
4 egg yolks
5 heaping tablespoons cornstarch

1 tablespoon vanilla
1 square unsweetened chocolate
1 can of cherries or peach slices
1 cup chopped walnuts
Decorating icing (See recipe in
this book) or whipped cream
Good-quality rum

Method

1. Beat yolks until smooth.
2. Heat 3 cups of the evaporated milk mixture.
3. Add sugar mixed with cornstarch to warm milk.
4. Add remaining cold milk to beaten egg yolks.
5. Add egg mixture to warm milk mixture.
6. Cook until it thickens. The mixture must be stirred constantly.
7. The cream is cooked completely when volcanic-like bubbles burst at the surface.
8. Remove half the cream and set aside.
9. Add unsweetened chocolate to the cream remaining in the pot and melt it.
10. Allow yellow and chocolate cream to cool.
11. Place the cake it on turntable and cut into three slices, keeping the knife level;
    set top layers aside.
12. Place your thumb over the top of the bottle, and splash rum generously on the
    bottom layer.
13. Spread chocolate cream evenly over the bottom layer.
14. Place the second cake layer over the chocolate cream.
15. Splash the second layer with rum.
16. Place yellow cream on top of the second layer, reserving some cream.
17. Place canned cherries or peaches over yellow cream.
18. Place the third layer on top of the cream and fruit and splash with rum.
19. Seal the sides of the cake with reserved yellow cream; decorate the sides with walnuts.
    Let the cake sit overnight if possible.
20. Frost with decorating icing or whipped cream, and let sit at least two hours
    in refrigerator.

My favorite birthday cake!

STARLIGHT CAKE

Ingredients

    2 cups plus 2 tablespoons flour
    1-1/2 cups sugar
    3-1/2 teaspoons baking powder
    1 teaspoon salt
    1/2 cup shortening
    1 cup milk
    1 teaspoon vanilla
    3 eggs
    Decorating icing (See recipe in this book)

Method

1.   Grease and flour two 8" cake pans.
2.   Sift flour, sugar, baking powder, and salt together.
3.   Mix shortening, milk, and flavoring for 2 minutes at medium speed.
4.   Add eggs and beat for an additional 2 minutes.
5.   Add dry ingredients.
6.   Bake at 350 degrees for 30 minutes or until golden brown. An inserted toothpick should come out clean.
7.   Allow cake to cool on rack before frosting. Frost with decorating icing.

Here's a picture is of a cakc that I decorated for my grandson's birthday. The theme was "curious creatures."

WEDDING CAKE

Ingredients

4-1/2 cups sifted cake flour
1 teaspoon baking powder
1/2 teaspoon ground cloves
1/2 teaspoon cinnamon
1/2 teaspoon mace
1 pound shortening
1 pound brown sugar
10 eggs
1/2 pound candied cherries,
cut into halves
1/2 pound candied pineapple diced

1 pound dates cut up
1 pound raisins
1 pound currents
1/2 citron
1/2 pound candied lemon and
orange peel
1/2 nut meats chopped
1 cup honey
1 cup molasses
1/2 cup cider

Method

1. Pre-heat oven to 250 degrees.
2. Grease cake pans, line with heavy parchment or brown paper, and grease again. For large loaves bake in 8" by 4" by 3" pans.
3. Sift flour, baking powder, and spices together 3 times.
4. Cream shortening and sugar until fluffy.
5. Add eggs, fruit, nuts, honey, molasses, and cider.
6. Add flour mixture in small amounts, mixing well after each addition.
7. Bake large loaves about 4 hours for larger loaves and 2 hours for smaller loaves.
8. When cakes are cooled, soak with brandy.
9. After the cake has been soaked with brandy, wrap the cakes in wax paper and then in foil. Store the cakes in a cool, dry place to age.

This is best a year after it is made. The brandy the cake is soaked in preserves it! The aroma makes you want to have a piece every time you find the cake.

WHITE FRUIT CAKE

<u>Ingredients</u>

    2 cups flour
    1/2 teaspoon baking powder
    Pinch of salt
    1/2 pounds butter
    1/2 cup sugar
    3 eggs
    1/2 cup milk
    1 teaspoon vanilla
    2 small containers of candied cherries
    2 small containers candied pineapple
    1 pound golden raisins

<u>Method</u>

1.   Sift together flour, baking powder, and salt.
2.   In another bowl, cream butter with sugar.
3.   Add eggs.
4.   Add milk, alternating with flour mixture.
5.   Add vanilla. Then add fruit and raisins.
6.   Pour batter evenly into two loaf pans greased and lined with wax paper.
7.   Bake for one hour at 350 degrees.

This was a cake recipe that a relative gave my mother. We always enjoyed the cake at Christmas, and my mom continues to make it for us.

CANNOLI

<u>Ingredients</u>

Shells

18 ounces flour
3/4 teaspoon salt
2 tablespoons butter
5 teaspoons sugar
2 eggs
1/3 teaspoon salt
1-1/2 ounces sweet vermouth or Marsala wine
Oil for frying

Fillings

You can use the yellow cream from the rum cake recipe in this book to fill the cannoli. You can also use the filling from the ricotta pie recipe in this book.

<u>Method</u>

1.   Sift flour and salt.
2.   Break in eggs
3.   Add softened butter or shortening, and mix lightly.
4.   Dissolve sugar in Marsala and add to mixture.
5.   Toss on floured board; knead until dough is soft.
6.   Divide dough into two parts.
7.   Set in cool place for 30 minutes.
8.   Roll each part paper thin and cut into 4-inch squares.
9.   Wrap each piece around wooden or aluminum tubes.
10.   Press edges together.
11.   Drop several stacks at a time into hot oil.
12.   Cook 1 minute, turning to brown evenly.
13.   Drain and cool.

CAT PIE

<u>Ingredients</u>

    1-1/2 loaves of stale cake or bread
    Hot milk (enough to soften the cake or bread)
    1/2 cup sugar
    1 cup raisins
    1/2 teaspoon cinnamon
    1 teaspoon nutmeg
    3 eggs
    1/2 teaspoon salt
    3 apples, chopped
    Ready-made dough for 2 pie crusts, rolled out

<u>Method</u>

1.   Line a pie plate with half of the pie crust dough.
2.   Mix ingredients all ingredients together in a bowl.
3.   Pour mixture into pan.
4.   Cover with second pie crust.
5.   Bake at 350 degrees for 1 hour.

Where this recipe got its name I have no idea! In the late '50s, I remember walking down Salem Street in the North End of Boston. Down some stairs, there was a little Jewish bakery with sawdust all over the floor. For 10 cents, we would buy this cake, and we would eat it on the train on our way home to what my cousins used to call the country–Belmont, Massachusetts!

DANISH PASTRY APPLE BARS

Ingredients

    2-1/2 cups flour
    1 teaspoon salt
    1 cup shortening
    1/2 cup milk, approximately
    1 egg, separated
    1 cup cornflakes, crushed
    8 cups apples, peeled and diced/chopped
    3/4 to 1 cup of sugar
    1 teaspoon cinnamon

Method

1. Combine flour and salt; cut in shortening.
2. In a measuring cup, beat egg yolk
3. Add enough milk to equal 2/3 of a cup of liquid and mix well.
4. Add egg mixture to flour mixture.
5. Roll out 2/3 of the dough to fit the side and bottom of greased 9" by 13" pan.
6. Place crushed cornflakes on top of crust.
7. Mix sugar and cinnamon (using enough of each to taste), and toss with apples.
8. Put apple mixture on the cornflakes.
9. Place top crust and brush with egg whites.
10. Bake at 375 degrees for 25 minutes.

An apple a day is good, but these pastry bars are absolutely luscious!

FRUIT TART

Ingredients

Cake:

6 eggs, separated
1 cup sugar
1 teaspoon vanilla
2 heaping teaspoons baking powder
1 cup flour
Fruit (kiwi, berries, peaches)
1/2 cup golden apple jelly

Cream:

1 can evaporated milk and water to equal one quart
1-1/2 cup sugar
4 egg yolks
5 heaping tablespoons cornstarch
1 tablespoon vanilla

Method

Cake:

1. Line two 8" round pans with waxed paper.
2. Beat egg whites until foamy.
3. Slowly add egg yolks to egg whites, one at a time.
4. Then add sugar and vanilla.
5. Add baking powder to flour and gradually fold them into the other ingredients.
6. Pour half the batter into each round tart pan.
7. Bake at 350 degrees for 15 to 20 minutes.
8. Remove from pan, cool on rack, and remove waxed paper.

Cream:

9. Beat yolks until smooth.
10. Heat 3 cups of the evaporated milk mixture.
11. Add sugar mixed with cornstarch to warm milk.
12. Add remaining cold milk to beaten egg yolks.
13. Add egg mixture to warm milk mixture.
14. Cook until it thickens.
15. This mixture must be stirred constantly to avoid burning the cream or pan.
16. The cream is cooked completely when volcanic-like bubbles burst at the surface.
17. Spread cream onto cooled cake. (You can drizzle liqueur on the sponge cake before adding the cream).
18. Decorate with fruit of your choice.
19. Melt the apple jelly in a sauce pan, and brush over the fruit. This prevents it from drying out or browning.

The secret to sponge cake is that the eggs need to be at room temperature. It can also be soaked in a liqueur. When you serve this dessert, you serve up some sunshine!

LEMON SQUARES

Ingredients

    2-1/2 cups flour
    1 teaspoon salt
    1 cup shortening
    1 egg, separated
    1/2 cup milk (approximately)
    2-1/2 cups flour
    1 teaspoon salt
    1 cup shortening
    1 package lemon filling, cooked as directed

Method

1. Combine flour and salt; cut in shortening.
2. In a measuring cup, beat egg yolk
3. Add enough milk to equal 2/3 of a cup of liquid and mix well.
4. Add egg mixture to flour mixture.
5. Roll out 2/3 of the dough to fit the side and bottom of 9" by 13" pan.
6. Pour lemon filling into bottom crust.
7. Place top crust and brush with egg whites.
8. Bake at 375 degrees until golden brown.

For fig squares, you can substitute fig filling that comes in a jar.

This recipe came from my mom's cooking class, and you can bet the students always sampled them before leaving class.

RICOTTA PIE

Ingredients

1 batch of Easter cookie dough recipe (See recipe for Easter basked cookies in
this book)
1 pound ricotta cheese
4 eggs
1/2 cup sugar
Vanilla

Method

1. Mold dough into two balls, dust with flour, and place each ball between two pieces
   of waxed paper.
2. Roll out the dough and place one piece on a glass pie plate.
3. Roll an egg around the raw dough. This seals the dough and makes the crust firmer.
4. Mix ricotta, eggs, sugar, and vanilla in a bowl. Don't beat—just blend.
5. Place the other piece of rolled-out dough on top.
6. Bake in a 350-degree oven for an hour.

This rich ricotta pie was always an Easter favorite, and it was always homemade for us. When
we were older, we got the chance to sample pie that was bought in the North End at Mike's
pastry shop. Although theirs looked different, it tasted the same.

It's the dough that makes the pie like no other. Delicious!

SICILIAN FRUIT BARS

Ingredients

    Crust:

    1-1/3 cups flour
    1/4 cup sugar
    1/2 cup butter, softened

    Filling:

    7 ounces of your favorite jam
    3/4 cup sugar
    2 eggs
    2 tablespoons flour
    1/4 teaspoon baking powder

Method

1. Pre-heat the oven to 350 degrees.
2. Mix the crust ingredients together at low speed until the mixture is crumbly.
3. Press into the bottom of an 8" square pan.
4. Bake 14-20 minutes or until the edges are golden brown.
5. Combine all of the filling ingredients.
6. Pour over the hot crust and bake an additional 15-20 minutes or until the filling is set.
7. Sprinkle with powdered sugar while warm and again when cooled.
8. Cut into 16 bars.

Sicilian fruit bars always get lots of compliments.

Although my mom never had a cooking show on television and I never before wrote a book of any kind, we both have something to share. My mother loves to cook, and I like to create art, whether it's an expression on paper or on canvas.

I married an Italian who left Italy at age 19, and he still goes back to visit his family every year in August, which is the time of feasts and celebrations. I have gone back with him quite a few times and have learned more about my own heritage and what I have missed about being Italian. When I visit, we usually stay in or around the town of San Donato. I am always taken aback by the beauty of the land and always see something new, even if it is old.

My sister-in-law has a farm about two miles into the mountains where she goes every morning. As she begins her journey, she stops halfway to change her clothes and puts on rubber boots, an apron, and a scarf on her head. She has a walking stick that helps her up hill that she also uses to fend off any snakes that might be in the dirt road. Her gate key hangs on her apron strings and lets her into the garden of plenty. There she feeds the chickens and rabbits, and any leftovers from yesterday's meals are for the cats. The cats chase away anything like foxes that might try to get the chickens. I went with her to the farm and helped out as much as I could, carrying the vegetables and eggs back to use that day for dinner. I will never forget what an adventure it was and wish my grandchildren could someday see how life is there.